INTRODUCTION

Welcome

Welcome to the Serengeti Tour Guide Tanzania book.

It all started after completing my full term of office as a legislator at the East African Community and returning to my hometown at Nyalikungu Maswa. I was visited by a group of students from a nearby Secondary school who wanted me to share my experience serving at the Legislative Assembly. Few years back there was a widely publicized tour of the Serengeti National Park by members of the Assembly. Among other things the visiting students wanted me to share was about the tour at Serengeti and how is Serengeti today. Millions of people have heard or visited the Serengeti since the production of the famous book and film by Grzimeks, *Serengeti Shall Never Die* some sixty years ago. A new film was launched in New York on 18th April 2022 by President Samia Suluhu Hassan of Tanzania, *Tanzania –The Royal Tour-* which also covers Serengeti today extensively.

I am not only an experienced safari traveler but a devoted lover of nature. I had traveled across Serengeti ecosystem many times since I was a teenager some forty plus years ago. Serengeti is only 100 kilometers from my hometown and my father used to grow maize at the Serengeti borderline at Matongo Village. Not many people forget their first encounter and subsequent visit to Serengeti. Maybe it is because of the seemingly endless grasslands stretching as you enter the Naabi Hill Gate or maybe the spectacular scene of wild animals in millions migrating in a circular pattern within the Serengeti ecosystem following seasonal changes and in search of greener pastures. Whatever it may be, 'karibu sana', the Kiswahili word for welcome, my visiting students and prospective tourists around the world to share my lifelong encounter to one of the greatest wildlife-watching destinations on earth. Hence, I hope you may find this narration a useful guide to your planned first or future tour to the Serengeti in 2022 and beyond.

I also covered specific information on plants and animals that are usually seen there. Most plants I mentioned during the conversation have no English names and hence referred to scientific names in the description. I did not use scientific names on animals because most have common English or Kiswahili names. The guide is independent publication and any opinion expressed are of the author and not of any Serengeti National Park authorities. I hope you will find the guidebook handy and enriching your tour aspirations.

General description

Whenever the name 'Serengeti' is mentioned it invokes an image of vast open plains with *Acacia* trees spread over the plains and with lions and other wild animals scouting the horizon, of hyenas squabbling at a carcass and of vultures soaring high above the sky.

The original Maasai word 'Siringet'- means an extended area where the land goes on forever. What makes Serengeti unique is the stage shifts with the seasons in a clockwise rotational manner as wild animals migrate with the main players remaining the same- the migratory zebra and wildebeest, predators and scavengers.

The bimodal rain pattern of East Africa makes that there are two rainy seasons in the period from November to May. The short rains are from November to December and are brought on by the northern monsoon. The long rains are brought on by the south-eastern monsoon and the last from February/March to May, with a short period of low rainfall or no rainfall during January and early February. The annual rainfall varies from _+500mm in the south-east to _+1,200mm in the north-west. Temperature is relatively uniform throughout the year with maximum temperatures of around 28 degrees centigrade whereas the minimum temperature in May to August is about 13 degrees centigrade. Extreme heat and extreme cold weather is exceptional rare at Serengeti National Park.

The Serengeti's close to 3,000 lions is probably the largest number of lions found in any national park in the world. Lions gorge themselves on wildebeest as they migrate from the east and once the migration reaches the western part of Serengeti in the Grumeti River area where animals need to cross on their route north, crocodiles are lurking.

Today, this migratory herd of animals is the largest remaining on earth. Though the natural phenomenon of the migration contributes to the fame of the Serengeti but hills, valley, lakes, rivers that feed Lake Victoria (the source of the Nile) and the variety and number of wild creatures and vegetation undeniably place Serengeti at its own league of national parks in the world.

How to get to the Serengeti National Park

They are different ways one can get to Serengeti National Park. You can fly to Kilimanjaro International Airport at Moshi, Tanzania, which is situated at the foot of Mount Kilimanjaro. From there you can take a chartered flight directly to Serengeti. Alternatively, there are shuttle bus service which will take you to Arusha City which is 55km away. At Arusha, you can hire a 4WD van from Tour Service Operators and drive 260km to the Serengeti entrance gate at Naabi Gate. On your way to Serengeti you will pass through the Ngorongoro Conservation area where the famous Ngorongoro Crater is located.

At Naabi Gate you pay entrance fees and given your time and schedule, you can take a walking trail up the hill to have a glimpse of the surrounding area. From Naabi, you can proceed to Seronera which is 58km away or to Lake Ndutu at which you will drive back 4km along the Ngorongoro Road, then 15km west where you will find the Lake.

History and People

It is believed that the presence of Tsetse fly, the host of virus that cause disease in animals and man is the reason why the history of the people that inhabited the Serengeti is not well known. However, it is said that Watindiga (Hadzabe) and the Maasai occupied Serengeti before leaving as recently as 1959.

Hadzabe or Watindiga tribe live near Lake Eyasi today. They were hunter-gatherers, hunting by means of bows and poisoned arrows. The Hadzabe speak a click language, are of high cheekbones, of light skin and smoke bone pipes. Evidence from cultural sites indicate their presence along the Mbalageti river in the Western Serengeti.

About 200 year ago the Maasai moved into the Serengeti/Ngorongoro area, probably in search of grazing for their cattle. From the late 1890s the Maasai were severely affected by Rinderpest, drought, famine, and locust. In 1958, a Treaty was signed in which their right to graze their cattle in the Serengeti was cancelled and were relocated to the Ngorongoro Conservation Area.

In 1951, Serengeti was formally gazetted as a national park with an area of around 25,500 square km. In 1981 the Serengeti National Park, was declared a World Heritage site.

PLACES TO SEE

Ndutu

Ndutu is one of the prime destinations in the Serengeti especially during the months because between December and May where wildebeest calve here and the migratory animals concentrate on the Short Grass plains to start the migration. This scene is interspersed by occasional gallops and much snorting. By the end of the year the migration will have come to full circle returning to these plains.

Apart from the well-located National Parks campsites, one place you can stay in this area is Ndutu Safari Lodge, which is just outside the park. When I was making a documentary for our local TV some years back, witnessed an exhilarating experience at Lake Ndutu where a group of about 50 wildebeest stampeded across the lake upon been triggered by an approaching cheetah. I gathered that the reason they run across the lake is because it is shallow and the distance to the other side is short.

Until they too join the migration, gazelle is in abundance at Ndutu short-grass plains stretching from the main road to a small, seasonal lake enclosed by acacia trees. Giraffes

and predators also reside in the area. Local guide told me that some years back wildebeest and zebras used to swim across Lake Ndutu. As for birdwatchers, the lake site is an attractive paradise.

Moru and Simba *Kopjes*

Moru (Maasai for "old") and Simba (Swahili for "lion") Kopjes are situated further north on the path of the migration as the wildebeest and accompanying zebras and gazelles begin to group and start their annual pilgrimage. Serengeti's surviving rhinoceros are also sighted in this area.

Moru and Simba Kopjes is a good area for game viewing throughout the year due to the availability of water. However, because of the slippery black cotton soil at this locality, access during the rainy season can be somewhat difficult.

There are evidence that Maasai pastoralists still lived in this area as recently as in 1950s. On one of the kopjes there I saw rock paintings which suggest that fact. When I last visited the kopjes with the paints two years ago, the paintings

The kopjes rising from the plains provide ample shade for prides of lion. They also provide a perfect observation points from which they search for their next meal. The best time of the year to visit Moru is from March to June, when the migration is likely to be passing through.

Serengeti Sopa Lodge is located this area and the Park Authorities have limited development in the area to ensure minimal disruption of the environment.

Kirawira

Kirawira also known as the Western Corridor, experience dry spell during June to October, the months I recommend you to visit this area. However, there is year-round resident game at Kirawira. There are many Cheetahs, lions, hyenas and leopards in this area. The corridor extends from west to northwest of Moru and almost joins Lake Victoria at the Ndabaka Gate through which you can reach Mwanza 140km away.

Through here the migrating herds pass in June and July every year. The Grumeti River flowing into Lake Victoria bisects the area where both crocodiles and hippopotamus are in hundreds. Black-and-white colobus monkeys and many species of birds can be seen in the riverine forest along the Grumeti River. There is a resident wildebeest population that annually watches the migration go past. Also present are large herds of topi unique to East Africa, giraffe and buffalo.

There are number of upmarket tented camp sites and where you can stay in this area.

Seronera

Seronera is the most important tourist destination in the Serengeti because its accessibility and modest infrastructure. From the south and central plains, the migrating herds cut across the park towards the northeast, passing through Seronera and outside the park's western boundary in the area of the Fort Ikoma Gate.

The Seronera River flows from the open plains in the southeast into the woodlands in the west. Seronera forms a transitional zone between open grassland in the south-east and the wooded grassland in the north-west. It is one place you can view virtually all resident animals such as lion, cheetah, leopard, spotted hyena, jackal, fox, giraffe, buffalo, topi, waterbuck, elegant Grant's and Thomson's gazelle, impala, reedbuck, dikdik, hippopotamus, warthog, baboon, monkey, hyrax and variety of reptiles and birds.

Seronera is a good place to visit throughout the year. Most camping sites are located in this area. Seronera Wildlife Lodge and Serengeti Serena Safari Lodge are also located here.

Lobo

Rich in water sources, Lobo area consists of vegetation types that support a variety of game. Ngare Naironya Springs and Upper Grumeti River provide sufficient water for the migratory and resident animals. From the center of the Serengeti, the migration heads north in June/July into this area and south again to return to the Short Grass plains. Klipspringers and impala are common in Lobo on the kopjes Other common game such as giraffe, elephants, hartebeest, gazelle and warthog are found in Lobo throughout the year. Lobo area is known for high concentrations of lions

Lobo Wildlife Lodge is the major facility for visitors to stay in this area. It is sculpted out of a rock kopje and lies along the migration route. Migration Camp with luxury tents is another good facility that takes advantage of this route. When members of the East African Legislative Assembly and I spent a night at Lobo Wildlife Lodge some ten years ago, the hospitality was memorial. Though I have travelled extensively across the continents, I have never to date experienced such splendid hotel service elsewhere.

Short Grass Plains

The Short Grass Plains of Serengeti is probably the only one place on earth where close to two million wild animals assemble and get natural support during the rainy season. Tanzania has two rainy seasons, the short rains in November/December and the long rains from March to May. As if sensing the rains, or maybe through sight (darkening skies and lightening) and thunder, the migration turns, heading south back into the Serengeti.

The first drops of rain bring lush green grass to the parched plains. This creates rich grazing areas for the migration and food for millions of insects that in turn attracts countless migratory birds.

Like a multiple New York marathon rally, the close to two million animals cross the Orangi River heading back to the south of Serengeti where they began, past Barafu and Gol kopjes. They will remain in the Naabi Hill and Ndutu area before beginning the cycle once again.

THE MIGRATION

Until I ventured to produce a TV documentary on Serengeti – 'Serengeti Today' in 2003, I still did not know where the migration would be in a given time. The migration is circular and for the purpose of this guide, the migration is considered to begin in January in the southeast of the Serengeti in Ndutu area near Naabi Gate. It has been observed over many years that the migration of animals at Serengeti is dictated by the seasons that bring rain and new grass. It has been observed that should the short rains fail or delay, the migration begins later. Likewise, should there be plenty of rains, the migration may not leave the Serengeti for Maasai Mara.

According to David Martin on 'SERENGETI' in 2005, no one knows for sure why does the migration occur at all. However, the timing and pattern of the migration activities lead to a number of interpretations.

Wildebeest are the dominant grass-eaters of the Serengeti. They take more grass per mouthful than any competitor. Therefore, huge concentration of wildebeest and attendant species swiftly exhaust grasslands and must move on for their survival. They set out on a continuous annual circuit in a perpetual march for better grazing and water sources as one area after another is exhausted.

It has been observed that wildebeest are extremely sensitive to rainstorms moving in their direction where fresh grazing is assured. Distant thunder also draws the herds which suggests the hearing and possibly vibration, is important although sight appears to be the principle sense.

The Serengeti contains many mysteries, not least of which is the response by visitors as to their main reasons for going to the national park in the first place. According to David Martin, the unique migration in which close to 2 million wildebeest, zebra and gazelle participate, ranks only sixth. Ahead of this, visitors list their motivation as seeing lion, cheetah, leopard, elephant and crocodile/hippocampus.

According to Veronica Roodt (2005) on 'Travel and Field Guide of the Serengeti National Park', migratory herds at Serengeti follows a general pattern with minor or sometimes major deviations as follows;

Early dry season (July to October). The bulk of the migratory herd is in the western corridor, and cross the Grumeti and Mara rivers in about July/August. During September and October, some enter Maasai Mara Game Reserve in Kenya.

Late dry season to early wet season (November to December). In the late dry season, the migratory herd starts its movement towards south through Lobo area and along the eastern borderline. Some move straight through Seronera. Most herd reach Short Grass Plains by mid-January. They have their offspring in February and March.

Early wet season (January to March). During this time the herd is mainly on the Short Grass Plains west of Gol Mountains in Ngorongoro Conservation Area, at Gol Kopjes, Barafu Kopjes, Naabi Gate and Lake Ndutu.

Late wet season (April to June). During this time, with first signs of rain, the herd starts a move following the green vegetation to the northwest plains along Seronera and Nyabogati rivers to the western corridor where they reach in June.

From the calendar of the migration outlined you can see that the migration is circular and almost perpetual. This guide prescribes the migration beginning in January in southeast of Serengeti in the Ndutu area near Naabi Gate.

WALKING AND BALLOON SAFARIS

Walking safaris has been introduced quite recently. Multiday camping trips are available at Kogatende along Mara River in the Moru Kopjes, and in other areas of the park. Lately, more sites are being sought for walking safari ventures. You may request more information in his regard as you plan your visit to Serengeti. I found the walking safaris more relaxing and adventurous than sitting in a 4WD vehicle watching.

One of the memorable experience you can hope to have in the Serengeti is a balloon ride. This is where you experience the sensation of feeling floating over the plains of Serengeti at dawn, then followed by a champagne breakfast in the bush under an acacia tree has been a better way to see the wonderful Serengeti. Taking typically one hour, you will rise to 1000m for a vast view, then drop to treetop level.

PREDATORS

Lion or 'Simba' in Kiswahili

The Serengeti probably host the largest lion population in Africa. The current estimates (2022) put it at about 3,000. Males reach their prime at the age of five or six years at which they have the ability to take over a pride from an older male. Two brothers normally remain together making it easier to oust another dominant male. When they take over a pride they chase away or even kill the young cubs and some of the older ones. It is touchy to see how the female in vainly try to defend cubs or try to lead them away.

With cubs out of way, the female almost immediately become ready to mate. The males rarely hold on to a pride for longer than three years, usually shorter. Strangely in a pride, lions are very sociable animals and they love to play, jointly hunt together, share their meals and protect their territories. The females of a pride are often related and it is not unusual for female of the same pride to suckle each other's cubs.

Lions hunt mainly at night but are easily seen during the day resting. At Serengeti, lions may be heard roaring at night and very rare during the day.

Lions are sluggish animals, showing an aversion to exerting themselves except when intent on a kill. Even then they can be inefficient, certainly when compared to hyena, and intended prey may bear morning-after scars showing where lions have hit and missed.

At Serengeti you will find lions lolling about or sleeping in the shade under trees or shrubs usually in prides or in small all-male of the same age groups. However, their apparent seemingly passiveness can swiftly turn into aggressiveness if disturbed, wounded or otherwise remotely threatened.

Prides position themselves close to their meal, that is where there is abundant game, such as buffalo, zebra and wildebeest. The lioness commands a special role and status in a pride although there may also be a dominant male.

Male lions become sexually mature at the age about two years but usually have to wait another three years to mate. Female become pregnant for the first time around the age of four and produce litters every two years until they are about 15 years old.

The average weight of an adult male lion is around 200kg, with females averaging 130kg.

The colour of adult is somewhat sandy or tawny on the upper body and white underneath. The backs of the rounded ears are black in sharp contrast to the body colour. The tail, roughly half the length of the combined head and body, can in some lions be black-tipped.

Adult males have a mane up to 16 cm in length that, with advanced years the mane can become black. The mane of the younger males tends to be sandy or tawny although climatic variations can affect the colour. Male lions without having mane are very rare.

Lions have five toes on the front feet and four on the rear one. Each toe has very sharp, scimitar-shaped, retractable claws. These claws, and the formidable lower jaw, are the main killing machinery.

Male lions rarely participate in the hunt, leaving this to the lioness. But once a kill is made they take the first priority, with the lionesses having to wait until the male has eaten his fill. Strangely, the cubs come last.

Cheetah or 'Duma' in Kiswahili

The cheetah is the fastest land animal which is capable to sprint at +120kph, but can only maintain that speed for about 100m. The difference between Cheetahs and other cats is that they are not able to retract their claws. Cheetahs are able to climbs tree vertically and the claws do give them extra grip when they sprint.

Their spinal cord is extremely flexible and stretch more than that of any other sprinting animal. Theoretically, it can be calculated that a cheetah would be able to run 'caterpillar-style' at 10km an hour, based only on the spine's ability to stretch and retract. Their population in Serengeti is estimated at about 500.

Leopard or 'Chui' in Kiswahili

There are many Leopards in Serengeti but because of their nocturnal nature, they are hardly seen. Leopards prefer heavily wooded areas, hills, kopjes and riverine forest. Therefore, it is obvious there are commonly sighted in Seronera and Lobo areas.

Leopard spend much of their time in trees and are capable of taking a middle-sized antelope up into a tree with little effort. They do this to secure their prey from other predators and scavengers. In the case that intestines of a prey fall to the ground the leopard will painstakingly cover them with soil to conceal the smell. Leopards are solitary and adult males and female only associate during mating.

Hyena or 'Fisi' in Kiswahili

The Serengeti is basically the natural home of spotted hyena. Estimated at 10,000, Serengeti host the largest hyena population in the world. You can see packs of more than 40 hyenas strolling together. Their dens consist of several burrows in close proximity to each other. Though they spend most of the day sleeping they are active at night. Their common practice is scavenging and hunting at the same time. A dominant female is the leader of the pack, meaning it a matriarchal society.

Females are larger than males and the genitals of the both sexes look alike, females having a pseudo-penis. A hyena has the strongest jaws of all animals, thus being able to crush the bonus very effectively and therefore produce calcium-rich droppings that turn white when dry.

African Hunting Dogs or 'Mbwa Mwitu' in Kiswahili

The African Hunting Dog is one of the rarest predators in the Serengeti although there were fairly common on the plains during the 1960s. Today, Hunting Dogs are hardly seen in Serengeti.

Hunting dogs have a unique social system and their survival depends on large packs. Hunting Dog male offspring remain in the natal pack and the females emigrate. When the pack goes hunting at least one member of the pack remains at the den to look after the pups. All members partake in the raising of the pups. After a hunt each member will bring a portion of its food to the young ones. This feeding frenzy is accompanied by excited yelps and darting around. The decline of the dogs has been attributed by the unusually large population of lions and hyenas in the Serengeti who fight and kill them without protections.

Jackal or 'Mbweha' in Kiswahili

Another common sight on the Serengeti plains is Jackal. There are three species of Jackal found in the Serengeti, the black-backed, the side-striped and the golden colored. Side-striped jackal is rare, the Golden jackal occurs mainly on the short-grass plains, and the black-back jackal is the one most commonly seen.

Male and female jackals remain partners for life, which is rare among mammals. Cubs are born mainly in dens in July/ August and after six months they are already hunting on their own. They may stay, raising the next year's litter, regurgitating food, baby-sitting and standing guard. David Martin (1997) writes, "the jackals', screaming yell ending with a few dog-like yaps is another of the Serengeti's memorable sounds".

Bat-eared Fox or 'Mbweha Masikio Popo'

Bat-eared Fox is another dog-like animal that feed exclusively on termites. They listen for their prey by holding their large ears close to the ground. They eat mainly Harvester Termites but also insects, spiders, small rodents, reptiles, birds and fruits.

They have slim, black legs, tiny feet with five pads and long claws for digging Their tails are bushy, black in color at the top and tip. They weigh about 4kg and are 30 cm at the shoulder.

They have the distinction of having the largest number of teeth (46-50) of any non-marsupial mammal. Other carnivores have an average of 32 teeth. Although they have very sharp teeth, their mouth lacks elongated top and bottom molars that enable other carnivores to tear meat apart. They form pair bonds, often for life, and they live in underground burrows.

HERBIVORES

Elephant or 'Tembo' in Kiswahili

African elephants are the most recognizable of all mammals in the Serengeti. Their sheer physical mass of about 6,000kg for males and half that for females, and their cannonball-size droppings make them conspicuous.

They are commonly sighted in the northern parts of the park in the more wooded Lobo and Seronera areas. But large herds also exist at Ndutu and around Grumeti River.

The number of elephants in the Serengeti has increased in recent years and it is believed to currently exceed 2,000.

Elephants are sociable animals living in family groups dominated by an adult female (matriarch), her calves and a number of closely related females and their offspring. Elephants are normally extremely passive animals that show great curiosity and can peacefully pass within inches of a vehicle. But when animals are sick, injured or threatened, they can be aggressive and dangerous.

Elephants produce dropping every hour thus fertilizing the soil in the process. The fertilizing process is enhanced by the activity of dug beetles, which roll the dung into balls, lay their eggs in it and then bury the balls.

Elephants replace their teeth six times in their life time. New teeth are formed in the back of the mouth and the old teeth in the front of the mouth and the old teeth in the front of the mouth break off. Their roots are assimilated into the bone, almost in conveyor-belt fashion. Elephants chew by rolling their molars backwards and forwards, not sideways like other herbivores.

Giraffe or 'Twiga' in Kiswahili

Giraffe is the tallest animal in the world with adult males standing some five metres. Males weigh up to two tones and their scientific name means in Arabic as big as a camel and spotted like a leopard.

The Serengeti species is called the Maasai giraffe. It has irregular star-shaped markings covering almost the entire body and each has distinct individual patterns. They tend to become darker with age.

Because their diet is almost exclusively acacia, they are not often found outside areas where these trees exist that is around Seronera and Lobo areas. And because of their height they do not compete with other species for food.

They are mainly diurnal, resting in the shade during the heat of the day. They move in an unusual way. When walking, the two legs on one side swing almost simultaneously and their gallop is ungainly. Even so, they have been timed at 56 km/h. They are docile animals but vigorously defend their young against such predators as lions.

Giraffes form very loose associations, the bond between mother and her young being the strongest.

Buffalo or 'Nyati' in Kiswahili

Buffaloes are common in the Serengeti and occur throughout the park in wooded, tall grass areas with plently of water. They are almost exclusively grazers, preferring the leaves of tall grasses. They roam in very large territories and form herds of up to 2,000. Buffalo numbers in the Serengeti are estimated at 100,000.

Adult male buffalo weigh 800kg and stand 1.4metre at the shoulder. Their legs are strong and stocky to support their massive bodies. Their muzzles are short, hair fringed ears large and hanging as with domestic cattle, eyes watchful and baleful. Adult males have horns that can be massive and are set on top of a heavy head bone which they use to pound a victim.

They are inquisitive as well as aggressive and their preferred habitat, such as that found in the Lobo area, must offer plentiful grass, water (they drink at least twice daily) and shade. When wounded they are highly dangerous.

Hippopotamus or 'Kiboko' in Kiswahili

Hippos or 'Kiboko' in Kiswahili occur in fresh-water rivers and pools. Most of their day is spent in the water and at night they get out to feed almost exclusively on grasses. Because of their low energy expenditure and slow metabolism, their food intake is much lower (about 50%) relative to that of other herbivores. They eat about 130kg of food in one night, which takes an average of two days and two nights to digest. They do not ruminate.

A hippo cannot sweat, but when exposed to sunshine its skin secretes as reddish liquid which lower water loss and protects the skin against sunburn. That is why we see hippos turning pink in the sun. They can stay under water for about five minutes and even give birth under water. In the Serengeti hippos occur mainly in the perennial rivers such as the Grumeti, the Mara, the Mbalageti and in pools in the Seronera river.

But, unless one gets between the hippopotamus on land and the water, they are generally not aggressive, although females are very protective of their young. Their scientific name is Greek meaning water or river horse. I have seen people in my village who were attacked and injured by a hippo as they confronted hippos in one early morning as they were returning back to their pond after night grazing around peoples nearby farms.

Hippopotamus are the only truly amphibious, hoofed animals, feeding by night on dry land, where they can eat 60kg of grass in a session, mating and calving in the water.

Their ears, eyes and nostrils are set high on their heads allowing them to keep these faculties above water to sense danger. Their barrel-shaped bodies, short, stocky legs and broad faces make them unmistakable. Their skin is greyish-black, frequently marked with battle scars.

Their deep grunts and snorts are a notable part of the African night chorus.

Rhino or 'Kifaru' in Kiswahili

Black Rhinos are browser, that is they are leaf-eaters, and their pointed upper lip is perfectly adapted to selecting leaves. The white Rhino, with its wide lips, feeds on grass. White is in fact a corruption of the word 'wide' and there is no colour difference at all.

Few black rhinos are found in the Serengeti. They occur mainly in the Moru Kopjes area are very seldom seen. Rhinos do not ruminate and produce very course dung. They do not have front teeth but only molars at the back of the mouth. Rhinos in Serengeti are guarded 24/7 against poachers through the Black Rhino Protection program. Each rhino is fitted with a tracking device which is implanted in the horn. Their horns consist of a substance similar to compressed hair, therefore they do not feel any pain when the tracking device is implanted. This also explains why they do not experience pain when they are de-horned.

Warthog or 'Nguruwe Mwitu' in Kiswahili

Warthog is one of the most captivating and busy animal you will see at Serengeti.

Warthog has a short neck and a long tapering head ending in a blunt, rounded snout. On either side of the face there is a prominent wart and males that can be distinguished as they have four warts while females have only two. The canine teeth form prominent, jutting tusks that curve upwards and just above them bristles grow out of their faces sideways. When running, their tails are held erect, unlike bush pig whose tails point down.

Warthog is the only wild pig that mainly grazes, which it does during the rainy season when grasses are green. During the dry season they concentrate on uprooting rhizomes, bulbs and tubers and they may eat bones, soil and stones for minerals. Because of their short necks the usually graze on their knees. Adults enter their burrows backwards so that any threatening predator must confront their sharp horns that they can use effectively.

Warthogs do not ruminate, they often graze and root by standing on their calloused knees. They have a matriarchal social system but share home ranges with bachelors and solitary males, preferring savannah woodland. Since they have managed to secure a food source high in protein which is largely ignored by other animals-roots and bulbs, they can afford to spend more time sleeping. They are therefore diurnal and spend the night in burrows.

Antelope or 'Swala' in Kiswahili

Serengeti is home to almost 20 species of antelope of which the wildebeest is one. The largest antelope is the Patterson's eland which that weighs up to 900kg and stands 1.7 metres at the shoulder.

They are dull fawn in colour, often with vertical white stripes on their bodies. Older bulls tend to become blue-grey and calves are a reddish-brown. Both sexes have horns that are laid back, spiraled and ridged.

Their preferred habitat is shrub and grassland, and they are mainly browsers who feed at night when the vegetation has more moisture. They range over large areas, but are not territorial. In summer months they form large herds that may number several hundred.

They trot rather than gallop, fight vigorously to defend their calves and each other, sometimes resulting in fatalities. The low cholesterol content of their meat, is particularly valued.

You will the **Kongoni,** a Kiswahili word for **Coke's hartebeest and Topi** both of which are fast runners. Two other antelope you will see are the **Defassa waterbuck and Impala.** Two other smaller antelope to be found in the Serengeti are **Kirk's dikdik and Klipspringer.** Other species of antelope you are likely to see are the **Bush duiker, Cotton's oribi, Chanler's reedbuck and Bohor reedbuck and Greater kudu.** One antelope species you will see all over the Serengeti are the **Grand gazelle and Thomson's gazelle.**

Zebra or 'Pundamilia' in Kiswahili

No two zebras are marked alike. But the task of distinguishing them by naked eyes is practically not possible as they are estimated to be more than 300,000 in the Serengeti. Zebras are very successful as herbivore species. It is strange that their population was not affected by the Rinderpest outbreak century ago.

It is a mystery how Zebras in Serengeti have managed to maintain their number with increased competition from the expanding wildest population predation. Their strong social system and their adaptability partially account for their success as a species.

They are equally well adapted to feed on tall and short grasses, having both top and bottom incisors. This enable them to nip off tough grass stems and to feed on fresh, green grasses. Zebra do not ruminate and therefore the food passes faster through their digestive system and their dropping are courses.

REPTILES AND AMPHIBIANS

Nile Crocodile

The Nile Crocodile is the most common in Africa. In Serengeti Nile crocodiles are famous for their interception of the animal migration as thousands of wildebeest and zebras cross the Grumeti and Mara rivers on their way north into Maasai Mara. The average Nile crocodile is 2.5 metres to 3.5 metres long and the maximum length is about 6 metres.

They can weigh up to 1000kg and live for as long as 100 years. Crocodile normally open their mouth to regulate their body temperature.

Other reptiles and amphibians

At Serengeti, you can encounter variety of snakes (including venomous snakes), lizards, tortoise, terrapins, frogs and toads in various locations of the park. It is therefore important to take to have a local tour guide on your side particularly when on a walking safari.

BIRDS AND BUTTERFLIES

Serengeti is home more than 500 species of birds. Some of them are migratory Eurasian who are present in Europe during winter months from October to April.

The ostrich, currently estimated to 5,000 in the Serengeti is the largest bird you will see. Ostriches are flightless and male has a recognizable black and white plumage with a naked neck. Ostriches are fast runners reaching 70k per hour and maintain their pace for a long distance.

Other birds you will most likely see are cranes, vultures, eagles, Kori bustards, Fischer's lovebirds and many more.

At Serengeti you will also see butterflies and moths which are numerous and particularly those belonging from one of the major insect order- Lepidoptera. These include the Christmas butterfly, White spotted commodore and Empress swallowtail.

TREES, FLOWERS AND GRASSES

Serengeti ecosystem is rich in hundreds of tree species scattered throughout the Park. For the purpose of this guidebook, I will mention only few and the most likely locations you are going to see them.

Most common tree along the rivers include the Prickly Acacia, Numnum, Sandpaper bush, Croton, Strangler Fig, Wild Olive, Tamarind, Small Jujube, African Mangosteen, Honeysuckle tree, Cape Ash and Coffee-bean Strychnos.

Trees most common in broad-leafed woodland are Acacia hockii, Acacia nilotica, Velvet Bushwillow, Sausage Tree, Marula Tree, Indaba Tree, Wild Pear and Candelabra.

Tree commonly found at Kopje (rocky outcrop) include Umbrella Thorn, African Allophylus, Tree Euphorbia, False Marula, Dwarf Potato Bush and Kopje Hibiscus. In wooded grassland of Serengeti most common trees are the Green Thorn.

Grassland Orchard, Wild Sesame, Scarlet Hibiscus, Ink Flower, Yellow Spider Wisp, Black-eyed Susan, Sedge and Blue Water Lily are some of the wild flowers in the Serengeti.

Spike Grass, Red Oat Grass, Blue Buffalo Grass, Needle Grass, Goose Grass, Couch Grass, Turpentine Grass and Spear Grass are very common grass in Serengeti National Park.

WHERE TO STAY

According to *lonely planet,* there are nine public campsites in the Serengeti. Among these, six are located around Seronera, one at Lobo and the two others at Ndabaka and Forte Ikoma gates. All the campsite facilities have flush toilets installed and some two at Seronera have solar lighting, showers and kitchen. Furthermore, there are dozens of special campsites located in different parts of the Park charging night tariffs about double compared to the ordinary camps.

It is advisable to book well in advance through TANAPA at serengeti@tanzaniaparks.go.tz to secure placement at the public campsites.

There number of private lodges and tented camps located inside and outside the park. They include Balili Mountain Resort, Dunia Camp, Grumeti Serengeti Tented Camp, Ikoma Tented Camp, Kirawira Camp, Klein's Camp, Lamai Serengeti, Ndutu Safari Lodge, Olakira Camp, Robanda Safari Camp, Sasakwa Lodge, Serengeti Bushtops Camp, Serengeti Migration Camp, Serengeti Serena Safari Lodge, Serengeti Sopa Lodge, Serengeti Stopover, Twiga Resthouse and Wayo Geen Camp. It is expected more facilities for sleeping and eating will be built in future.

LANGUAGE

Kiswahili is the national language in Tanzania as well as in neighboring Kenya. Only recently the United Nations has designated 7th July to be the World's Kiswahili Day. Currently it is spoken throughout East Africa and increasingly being taught in many Universities around the world including the US.

I strongly advise you to familiarize with some Kiswahili words and phrases as you plan to visit Tanzania and Serengeti in order to ease communication with local service providers. Herewith I suggest some of the words and phrases you can begin acquainting with:

'Jambo' - means How are you?

'Habari' – also How are you?

'Shikamoo' – also How are you (referred to an elder party)

'Tafadhali' – Please…

'Asante' - Thank you

'Karibu sana' – You are warmly welcome

'Samahani' – Excuse me or sorry

'Nzuri or Salama or Poa' – I am fine or I am OK

'Jina lako nani?' – What's your name?

'Jina langu ni..' – My name is …

'Chumba ni bei gani?' – How much is a room?

'Utakunywa chai au kahawa?' – Will you have tea or coffee?

'Naomba bili' – Can I have the bill, please?

'Tunakwenda wapi?' – Where are we going?

'Nitafikaje huko?' – How do I get there?

'Saidia' - Help

'Toka' - Get away

'Naweza kununua?' – Can I buy

'Ni ghali sana' – It is too expensive

'Ni saa ngapi sasa?' – What is the time now?

OK, continue learning more Kiswahili words and sentences, you will be fine.

CONCLUSION

I hope you found reading this guidebook handy and helpful. I will appreciate if you will recommend it to other prospective Tanzania and Serengeti tourists, and nature loving enthusiasts around the world and review the book on Amazon.

You are welcome to Serengeti, Karibu sana Tanzania.

REFERENCES

Martin, D. (1997). *Serengeti Tanzania: Land, people, history (Into Africa travel guide)* (Reprinted 2005 ed., Vol. 1). Tanzania National Parks.

Roodt, V. (2005). *The Tourist Travel & Field Guide of the Serengeti* (Vol. 1). Papyrus Publications.

Fitzpatrick, M., Bartlett, R., Else, D., Ham, A., & Smith, H. (2018). *Lonely Planet Tanzania 7 (Travel Guide)* (7th ed., Vol. 1). Lonely Planet.

Printed in Great Britain
by Amazon